SECRETS TO BUILD A SUCCESSFUL CAREER

THE STEPS TO ACHIEVING PROFESSIONAL SUCCESS

DR. JAGADEESH PILLAI

*|| Dedicated to all wisdom seekers around
the world ||*

Contents

Contents

Prayer

**"Om Bhadram Karnebhih Shrunuyaama
DevaahBhadram Pashyemaakshabhiryajatraah
SthirairangaistushtuvaamsastanoobhihVyashema
Devahitam YadaayuhSwasti Na Indro
VridhashravaahSwasti Nah Pooshaa
VishwavedaahSwasti Nastaarkshyo ArishtanemihSwasti
No Brihaspatir DadhaatuOm Shantih, Shantih, Shantih"**

The literal meaning of this mantra is: OM. O Gods! Let us hear auspicious words from our ears. O reverent Gods! Let us behold propitious visions from our eyes, let our organs and body be stable, healthy, and strong. Let us do that which is pleasing to the gods in the life span allotted to us. May Indra, inscribed in the scriptures, bring us fortune! May Pushan, the knower of the world, grant us prosperity! May Trakshya, who vanquishes enemies, bestow us with blessings! May Brihaspati bring us success!
OM Peace, Peace, Peace.

About The Author

Dr. Jagadeesh Pillai is a renowned Guinness World Record holder, writer, and researcher hailing from Varanasi, also known as the abode of Lord Shiva. With a Ph.D. in Vedic Science and a range of creative ideas and achievements, he is a true polymath. He is the author of more than 100 books including Research Publications. Although his roots can be traced back to Kerala, the people of Varanasi hold him in high regard and affectionately consider him one of their own.

In 1998, Dr. Pillai was offered a job at Banaras Hindu University, but he left the position after only two months to pursue greater goals in life. He believed that in order to study Indian scriptures and engage in other creative endeavours, he needed to retire from the daily grind of working solely for money at a young age.

He started an export business from scratch, using the knowledge he had gained from a previous job in the industry. His intelligence and unique approach to business led to great success in a short period of time, earning him more in just a decade and a half than he would have in a lifetime working in a government job. Upon the passing of Dr. APJ Abdul Kalam, Dr. Pillai decided to leave the business and dedicate himself to reading, studying, researching, and experimenting.

During his tenure in the export business, Dr. Pillai traveled to over 16 countries, gaining valuable insight and experiencing the world and life in detail.

Dr. Pillai has achieved four Guinness World Records in the following subjects:

"**Script to Screen**" - In this record, Dr. Pillai produced and directed an animation film within the shortest time possible, breaking the previous record set by Canadians. He has also received numerous national and international awards and recognitions for this achievement.

Longest Line of Postcards - For this record, Dr. Pillai created a line of 16,300 postcards on the occasion of the 163rd anniversary of Indian Postal Day. The event also included a questionnaire about the Indian flag.

Largest Poster Awareness Campaign - Dr. Pillai designed an awareness campaign on the subject of "Beti Bachao - Beti Padhao" (Save the Girl Child - Educate the Girl Child) to achieve this record.

Largest Envelope - In tribute to the Indian Prime Minister's "Make in India" initiative, Dr. Pillai created a 4000 square meter envelope using waste paper to achieve this record.

Attempted - **70000 Candles on a 210 kg Cake** - To celebrate the 70th Indian Independence Day, Dr. Pillai attempted to light 70,000 candles on a 210 kg cake, which was recorded in World Records India.

Attempted - **Documentary on Dhamek Stupa of Sarnath in 17 Languages** - Dr. Pillai attempted to create a documentary on the Dhamek Stupa of Sarnath, dubbing it in 17 different languages. The result of this attempt is currently awaiting confirmation from the Guinness World Records.

Dr. Pillai is skilled in teaching the Bhagavad Gita, a Hindu scripture, and is popular among young people. He has helped many young people improve their lives through his motivational teachings.

In addition to teaching, he has composed and sung numerous Sanskrit Bhajans and patriotic songs.

He has also written and directed several short films and documentaries for awareness campaigns, and has volunteered with the police in both UP and Kerala to spread awareness about various issues through videos and photography.

Incredibly, he has produced and directed over 100 documentaries about the city of Varanasi, all on his own.

He has also helped and guided more than 25 boys and girls to achieve world records through creative and innovative methods. He is a multifaceted person who uses his intellect and the blessings given to him by God to excel in various areas. He is both a teacher and a student, always learning and teaching, and is able to master any subject he comes across.

He is a selfless social activist and motivational speaker who has overcome struggles and failures to become a successful and enthusiastic individual with a rich life experience.

In addition to his work with the Bhagavad Gita, he is also

an efficient Tarot card reader, Astro-Vastu consultant, and a talented singer and composer. He has sung the entire Ram Charita Manas and Bhagavad Gita in his own compositions, and has sung the phrase "Lokah Samastha Sukhino Bhavantu" in 50 different languages. He is currently working on a detailed and scientific study of Vedas, Upanishads, Puranas, and the Bhagavad Gita. He has also composed and sung the Hanuman Chalisa and Gayatri Mantra in 108 and 1008 different compositions, respectively.

Awards - Four Times Guinness World Records, Winner of Mahatma Gandhi Vishwa Shanti Puraskar, Mahatma Gandhi Global Peace Ambassador, Kashi Ratna Award, Dr. APJ Abdul Kalam Motivational Person of the Year 2017, Mother Teresa Award, Indira Gandhi Priyadarshini Award, Bharat Vikas Ratna Award, Udyog Ratna Award, Vigyan Prasar Award, Poorvanchal Ratn Samman.

Preface

In today's rapidly changing job market, it's more important than ever to develop a successful career strategy. With the rise of automation, globalization, and the gig economy, the traditional career path is no longer the only path to professional success. That's why it's essential to be proactive in developing the skills, knowledge, and networks that will help you reach your career goals.||

This book, "Secrets to Build a Successful Career: The Steps to Achieve Professional Success," is designed to help you navigate the complex and constantly evolving job market. Drawing on the latest research and insights from experts in the field, this book provides practical advice on how to build a successful career, from developing your professional skills to negotiating your salary and benefits to planning your retirement strategy.

Whether you're just starting out in your career, looking to make a change, or seeking to advance to the next level, this book will help you chart a course for professional success. Whether you're looking to develop your leadership potential, enhance your professional image, or overcome career challenges, this book will provide you with the guidance and tools you need to reach your goals.

Through clear, concise, and actionable advice, this book will help you build the skills, knowledge, and networks you need to succeed in today's job market. Whether you're an entry-level employee, a mid-career professional, or an executive, this book will help you navigate the job market and achieve the career success you deserve.

BUILDING YOUR PROFESSIONAL NETWORK

Networking is a vital aspect of career success, and building a strong professional network can help you achieve your career goals. Here are the steps to build and maintain a successful professional network:

Identify your goals: Define what you want to achieve through networking, whether it is finding a new job, learning about a new industry, or making new connections.

Connect with people in your field: Attend industry events, join professional organizations, and connect with colleagues and classmates. Utilize LinkedIn and other professional social media platforms to expand your network.

Build meaningful relationships: When connecting with people, take the time to have conversations and get to know them. Follow up with them after events and offer to help with their professional endeavors.

Offer value: Share your knowledge and expertise, make introductions to other valuable contacts, and offer help whenever you can.

Stay in touch: Keep in touch with your network regularly, whether through emails, phone calls, or in-person meetings.

Be a valuable resource: Offer to help others in your network, provide information and resources, and be a source of support.

Give back: Volunteer for professional organizations and attend events to give back to your community.

Be authentic: Be yourself, and let your personality and values shine through in your interactions.

Remember, building a professional network takes time and effort, but the benefits are immense. A strong network can open doors to new opportunities, provide support and guidance, and help you achieve your career goals.

"Successful careers are not planned. They develop when people are prepared for opportunities because they know their strengths, their method of work, and their values."

- Harvey Firestone

CHAPTER TWO

DEVELOPING YOUR PROFESSIONAL SKILLS

Continuous learning and skill development is crucial for success in today's rapidly changing job market. Here are the steps to developing your professional skills:

Identify your strengths and weaknesses: Take stock of your current skills and areas that need improvement.

Set specific goals: Determine what skills you want to acquire or improve, and set specific, measurable goals to track your progress.

Seek out learning opportunities: Enroll in courses, attend workshops and conferences, read books and articles, and network with professionals in your field.

Practice and apply new skills: Find opportunities to apply your new skills on the job, and seek feedback from colleagues and mentors to continuously improve.

Utilize technology: Take advantage of online learning platforms, virtual workshops, and webinars to access a wealth of information and resources.

Seek mentorship: Find a mentor who can provide guidance, support, and constructive feedback to help you grow and develop in your career.

Stay up-to-date: Stay informed about the latest developments and trends in your field, and continuously seek out new learning opportunities.

Be flexible and adaptable: Be open to change and willing to learn new skills and technologies to stay ahead of the curve.

By continuously developing your skills and knowledge, you can increase your value to your employer and remain competitive in the job market. Remember, the more you invest in yourself, the more opportunities you will have to achieve professional success.

"Successful people do what unsuccessful people are not willing to do. Don't wish it were easier; wish you were better."

- Jim Rohn

CHAPTER THREE

LEVERAGING YOUR KNOWLEDGE AND EXPERIENCE

Maximizing the value of your knowledge and experience is key to advancing your career and achieving professional success. Here are the steps to leverage your knowledge and experience:

Reflect on your career:

Take the time to reflect on your experiences, achievements, and challenges to gain insights into your strengths and areas for improvement.

Identify transferable skills:

Analyze your skills and experiences to identify those that are transferable to other industries and roles.

Build a strong professional brand:

Develop a personal brand statement that showcases your unique skills and experience, and use it to market yourself effectively to potential employers and clients.

Network strategically:

Network with people in your field and beyond, and seek out opportunities to showcase your skills and experience.

Utilize social media:

Use social media platforms, such as LinkedIn, to build a strong online presence and connect with potential employers and clients.

Continuously learn and grow:

Seek out opportunities for professional development and continuously improve your skills and knowledge.

Share your expertise:

Publish articles, give presentations, and participate in professional organizations to share your knowledge and experience with others.

Be proactive:

Take initiative and seek out new opportunities to showcase your skills and experience, and demonstrate your value to your employer or clients.

By leveraging your knowledge and experience, you can increase your visibility and marketability, and advance your career to the next level. Remember, the more you invest in yourself and your career, the more opportunities you will have to achieve professional success.

"Success is not final, failure is not fatal: it is the courage to continue that counts."

\- Winston Churchill

CHAPTER FOUR

CRAFTING YOUR PROFESSIONAL BRAND

Your professional brand is the perception that others have of you based on your skills, experiences, and reputation. Here are the steps to crafting your professional brand:

Define your personal values and strengths: Identify the values and strengths that drive you, and use them to guide your professional development.

Analyze your target audience: Determine who your target audience is and what they value, so you can tailor your brand to meet their needs.

Develop your personal brand statement: Create a concise, compelling statement that summarizes who you are, what you do, and what sets you apart.

Consistently communicate your brand: Use your personal

brand statement in your resume, LinkedIn profile, and other professional communications to consistently communicate your brand.

Build your online presence: Use social media platforms, such as LinkedIn, to build a strong online presence and connect with potential employers and clients.

Network strategically: Network with people in your field and beyond, and seek out opportunities to showcase your skills and experience.

Seek out opportunities to showcase your brand: Volunteer for leadership roles in professional organizations, speak at conferences and events, and participate in industry groups to build your reputation and showcase your brand.

Continuously improve your brand: Continuously reflect on your personal brand, and seek feedback from colleagues and mentors to continuously improve.

By crafting a strong, authentic professional brand, you can increase your visibility and marketability, and position yourself for success in your career. Remember, the more you invest in your personal brand, the more opportunities you will have to achieve professional success.

"Success is where preparation and opportunity meet."

- Bobby Unser

CHAPTER FIVE

UNDERSTANDING CAREER GROWTH OPPORTUNITIES

Career growth opportunities are the stepping stones that lead you to success in your career. Here are the steps to understanding career growth opportunities:

Reflect on your career goals:

Identify your long-term career goals, and use them to guide your career growth plan.

Analyze your current position:

Assess your current role and responsibilities, and identify areas for growth and improvement.

Research your industry:

Stay up-to-date on industry trends and changes, and seek

out opportunities for professional development and advancement.

Network with industry leaders:

Connect with leaders in your industry, and seek out opportunities to learn from their experiences and insights.

Seek feedback from your supervisor:

Ask your supervisor for feedback on your performance, and use it to identify areas for improvement and opportunities for growth.

Utilize professional development programs:

Take advantage of professional development programs and training opportunities to build your skills and knowledge.

Seek out new opportunities:

Be proactive in seeking out new opportunities for growth, such as taking on new projects, seeking a new role within your organization, or exploring opportunities outside of your current company.

Continuously evaluate your progress:

Continuously reflect on your career growth, and seek out feedback from colleagues and mentors to evaluate your progress and identify opportunities for improvement.

By understanding career growth opportunities and taking

proactive steps to advance your career, you can achieve professional success and reach your career goals. Remember, the more you invest in your career, the more opportunities you will have for growth and success.

"Successful people are those who take
action. They make mistakes, but they don't
quit."

- John C. Maxwell

CHAPTER SIX

Mapping Out Your Career Journey

A career journey is the roadmap to success in your career. Here are the steps to mapping out your career journey:

Define your career goals: Identify your long-term career goals, and use them to guide your career journey.

Assess your current skills and experiences:

Reflect on your current skills, experiences, and accomplishments, and identify areas for improvement.

Research potential careers:

Research potential careers and industries, and identify those that align with your goals and interests.

Create a list of steps to reach your goals:

Based on your research, identify the steps you need to take to reach your career goals, such as acquiring new skills or gaining relevant experience.

Develop a timeline:

Create a timeline for your career journey, and establish deadlines for reaching each of the steps on your list.

Seek out mentors and advisors:

Connect with mentors and advisors in your field, and seek their guidance and support as you work towards your goals.

Monitor your progress:

Continuously monitor your progress and adjust your career journey as needed to stay on track.

Celebrate your accomplishments:

Celebrate your accomplishments and reflect on the lessons you've learned, and use them to continue to grow and succeed in your career.

By mapping out your career journey, you can have a clear roadmap for success in your career. Remember, the more you plan and invest in your career, the more opportunities you will have for growth and success.

"Successful people are always looking for opportunities to help others. Unsuccessful people are always asking, 'What's in it for me?'"

- Brian Tracy

CHAPTER SEVEN

Staying Motivated Throughout Your Career

Staying motivated is key to achieving success in your career. Here are the steps to staying motivated throughout your career:

Identify your motivation: Understand what drives you and what you are passionate about in your work.

Set achievable goals: Set realistic and achievable goals, and break them down into smaller, manageable steps.

Focus on progress: Celebrate your progress, no matter how small, and focus on what you've accomplished, rather than what you haven't.

Surround yourself with positive influences: Surround

yourself with positive, supportive people who believe in you and your goals.

Stay organized: Stay organized and prioritize your tasks to avoid feeling overwhelmed.

Take breaks and recharge: Take breaks when you need them, and engage in activities that recharge your batteries and help you stay motivated.

Stay curious and continuously learn: Stay curious, and continue to learn and grow in your career. Seek out new opportunities for professional development and learning.

Celebrate your successes: Celebrate your successes, both big and small, and use them to fuel your motivation and drive you towards your goals.

By staying motivated, you can overcome obstacles and achieve success in your career. Remember, success in your career is a journey, and staying motivated is key to reaching your goals.

"Successful careers are built through hard work and determination. You need to be willing to put in the time and effort required to reach your goals."

- Oprah Winfrey

CHAPTER EIGHT

HANDLING STRESS IN THE WORKPLACE

Stress in the workplace is a common challenge that can impact your productivity, well-being, and career success. Here are the steps to handling stress in the workplace:

Identify the sources of stress: Understand what is causing your stress and assess its impact on your work and personal life.

Develop coping mechanisms: Develop coping mechanisms, such as deep breathing, exercise, or mindfulness practices, to help you manage stress.

Communicate with your manager and colleagues: Communicate with your manager and colleagues about your workload and stress levels, and seek their support in managing stress.

Prioritize self-care: Prioritize self-care, and engage in activities that promote physical, emotional, and mental well-being.

Manage your workload: Manage your workload, prioritize your tasks, and avoid overcommitting yourself.

Practice good time management: Practice good time management, and allocate your time and resources effectively to minimize stress and maximize productivity.

Seek support from friends, family, and professional resources: Seek support from friends, family, and professional resources, such as counseling or therapy, to manage stress.

By handling stress in the workplace, you can maintain your productivity, well-being, and career success. Remember, taking care of yourself and managing stress is an ongoing process, and it's important to seek support when you need it.

"Success is a journey, not a destination. The doing is often more important than the outcome."

- Arthur Ashe

CHAPTER NINE

NEGOTIATING SALARY AND BENEFITS

Negotiating salary and benefits is a critical part of building a successful career. Here are the steps to negotiating salary and benefits:

Research market standards: Research the market standards for your industry and position to understand the typical salary and benefits package.

Prepare for the negotiation: Prepare for the negotiation by understanding your skills, experiences, and value proposition.

Focus on the outcome: Focus on the outcome of the negotiation, rather than just the salary or benefits offered.

Be flexible: Be flexible in your approach and open to alternative options, such as additional time off or flexible work arrangements.

Know your limits: Know your limits and be prepared to walk away if the offer does not meet your expectations.

Negotiate with confidence: Negotiate with confidence and be assertive in presenting your case.

Consider non-monetary benefits: Consider non-monetary benefits, such as additional training and development opportunities, that can have a long-term impact on your career.

By negotiating salary and benefits effectively, you can secure the compensation package that aligns with your skills, experiences, and career goals. Remember, negotiating salary and benefits is a process that requires preparation, confidence, and a willingness to be flexible.

"Success is not just about what you accomplish in your life; it's about what you inspire others to do."

CHAPTER TEN

BUILDING EFFECTIVE WORKING RELATIONSHIPS

Building effective working relationships is critical for professional success. Here are the steps to building effective working relationships:

Communicate effectively: Communicate effectively with your colleagues, manager, and clients, and listen to their perspectives and needs.

Be dependable: Be dependable and follow through on your commitments, and support your colleagues in meeting their goals.

Show appreciation: Show appreciation for your colleagues and their contributions, and acknowledge their strengths and accomplishments.

Be a team player: Be a team player and collaborate with others to achieve common goals, and seek to understand and respect different perspectives and opinions.

Build trust: Build trust by being transparent, honest, and reliable, and by keeping confidences and respecting others' privacy.

Seek feedback: Seek feedback from your colleagues and manager, and be open to constructive criticism and learning opportunities.

Foster a positive work environment: Foster a positive work environment by promoting teamwork, collaboration, and inclusiveness.

By building effective working relationships, you can create a supportive and positive work environment, increase your personal and professional growth opportunities, and enhance your professional success. Remember, building effective working relationships requires open communication, teamwork, and mutual respect.

"Success in a career is not about finding the right job, it's about creating the right job for yourself."

\- Richard Branson

CHAPTER ELEVEN

ENHANCING YOUR PROFESSIONAL IMAGE

Enhancing your professional image is important for building a successful career. Here are the steps to enhancing your professional image:

Dress appropriately: Dress appropriately for your industry and role, and invest in professional attire that reflects your personal brand.

Be professional: Be professional in your behavior, communication, and interactions, and maintain a positive attitude and demeanor.

Build your online presence: Build your online presence by creating a professional profile on LinkedIn, Twitter, and other social media platforms.

Network: Network with others in your industry, attend events and conferences, and seek opportunities to connect with others.

Develop your personal brand: Develop your personal brand by defining your values, strengths, and areas of expertise, and communicating your value proposition to others.

Seek professional development opportunities: Seek professional development opportunities, such as training programs, workshops, and courses, to enhance your skills and knowledge.

Foster a positive attitude: Foster a positive attitude and seek out opportunities to develop and grow, and embrace new challenges and learning experiences.

By enhancing your professional image, you can communicate your value and build a strong personal brand that reflects your skills, experiences, and career aspirations. Remember, enhancing your professional image requires effort, dedication, and continuous learning and development.

"Successful people are not gifted; they just
work hard, then succeed on purpose."

- G.K. Nielson

Developing Your Leadership Potential

Leadership skills are critical for success in any career. Here are the steps to developing your leadership potential:

Identify your leadership style: Identify your personal leadership style by evaluating your strengths, weaknesses, and areas of opportunity.

Seek feedback: Seek feedback from your peers, colleagues, and managers to understand how you are perceived as a leader and identify areas for improvement.

Develop your skills: Develop your leadership skills through training, mentoring, and experience. Focus on areas such as communication, decision making, and strategic thinking.

Embrace change: Embrace change and be open to new ideas and approaches, and be willing to take risks and experiment with new strategies.

Lead by example: Lead by example and model the behaviors and values that you want your team to emulate.

Build and maintain relationships: Build and maintain relationships with your team, stakeholders, and customers, and work to build trust and credibility.

Foster a positive work culture: Foster a positive work culture by encouraging open communication, collaboration, and teamwork, and promoting work-life balance and wellness.

By developing your leadership potential, you can become a more effective and inspiring leader and drive success for your team and organization. Remember, leadership is a continuous learning journey, and it requires effort, dedication, and ongoing self-reflection and improvement.

*"Success is not the key to happiness.
Happiness is the key to success. If you love
what you are doing, you will be successful."*

- Albert Schweitzer

CHAPTER THIRTEEN

MANAGING TIME AND RESOURCES

Effective time and resource management is critical to success in any career. Here are the steps to managing time and resources effectively:

Set clear priorities: Identify the most important tasks and activities and focus your time and resources on them.

Plan your day: Plan your day by creating a to-do list, and prioritize tasks based on their level of importance and urgency.

Eliminate distractions: Eliminate distractions, such as email and social media, and focus on completing tasks with a single-minded focus.

Delegate effectively: Delegate tasks to others when appropriate, and trust them to complete them to a high standard.

Be flexible: Be flexible and willing to adapt your plans and priorities as circumstances change.

Stay organized: Stay organized and maintain clear systems for tracking your progress and tasks.

Manage stress: Manage stress by taking breaks, practicing mindfulness, and engaging in physical activity.

By managing time and resources effectively, you can maximize your productivity and achieve your goals more efficiently. Remember, it's important to be disciplined and focused, and to regularly assess and refine your time and resource management strategies.

"Successful careers are built through consistent effort, patience, and perseverance."

CHAPTER FOURTEEN

OVERCOMING CAREER CHALLENGES

No career journey is free of obstacles and challenges, but with the right approach, these challenges can be overcome and even become opportunities for growth and advancement. Here are the steps to overcoming career challenges:

Identify the challenge: The first step in overcoming any challenge is to clearly identify what the challenge is.

Assess the impact: Assess the impact of the challenge on your career, including the potential consequences and opportunities for growth.

Develop a plan: Develop a plan to address the challenge, including short-term and long-term goals, and actionable steps to achieve them.

Seek support: Seek support from trusted colleagues, friends, family, or a mentor. They can provide guidance, encouragement, and a fresh perspective on the situation.

Learn from experience: Learn from the experience of overcoming the challenge and use the lessons learned to improve your skills and abilities.

Stay positive: Stay positive and maintain a growth mindset, focusing on solutions and opportunities rather than dwelling on the challenge itself.

Be persistent: Be persistent and keep working towards your goals, even in the face of setbacks and obstacles.

By following these steps, you can successfully overcome career challenges and emerge stronger and more resilient. Remember, challenges are a natural part of the career journey, and with the right approach, they can be overcome and lead to even greater success and fulfillment.

"Successful people have fear, successful people have doubts, and successful people have worries. They just don't let these feelings stop them."

- T. Harv Eker

CHAPTER FIFTEEN

PLANNING YOUR RETIREMENT STRATEGY:

Retirement planning is an important aspect of building a successful career and achieving long-term financial security. Here are the steps to planning your retirement strategy:

Assess your financial situation: Assess your current financial situation, including your income, expenses, and debt. This will give you a clear understanding of your financial position and help you determine your retirement goals.

Determine your retirement goals: Determine your retirement goals, including the age at which you want to retire, your desired lifestyle, and the amount of money you will need to support that lifestyle.

Create a budget: Create a budget to help you manage your expenses and save for retirement. Be realistic about your expenses and consider ways to reduce your costs.

Start saving early: Start saving for retirement as early as possible, taking advantage of the power of compounding over time. Consider using a retirement savings plan, such as a 401(k) or an IRA, to help you save.

Consider additional sources of income: Consider additional sources of income, such as a part-time job or rental property, to help supplement your retirement savings.

Evaluate your investment portfolio: Evaluate your investment portfolio to ensure that it aligns with your retirement goals and risk tolerance. Consider working with a financial advisor to help you make informed investment decisions.

Plan for healthcare costs: Plan for healthcare costs, which can be significant in retirement. Consider purchasing a long-term care insurance policy or exploring alternative options, such as a health savings account.

Review your plan regularly: Review your retirement plan regularly and make adjustments as needed to ensure that you are on track to meet your goals.

By following these steps, you can create a solid retirement strategy that will help you achieve your financial goals and enjoy a comfortable retirement. Remember, the earlier you start planning for retirement, the more time you will have to save and invest, and the more secure your financial future will be.

"Success is not how high you have climbed,
but how you make a positive difference to
the world."

- Roy T. Bennett

Other Books Of The Author

1. The Moments When I Met God
2. Kashiyile Theertha Pathangal
3. GURU GYAN VANI
4. Abhiprerak Gita
5. ASSI SE JAIN GHAT TAK
6. Hopelessness of Arjuna
7. The Soul and It's True Nature
8. Sense of Action (Karma)
9. Action through Wisdom
10. Action through Wisdom
11. THEORY AND PRACTICAL OF EVERY ACTION
12. LOGICAL UNDERSTANDING OF THE SUPREME
13. THE IMPERISHABLE SUPREME
14. Yatra Nishadraj se Hanuman Ghat Tak
15. Yatra Karnatak Ghat se Raja Ghat Tak
16. Yatra Pandey Ghat se Prayagraj Ghat Tak
17. Yatra Ranjendra Prasad Ghat se Dattatreya Ghat Tak
18. YaatraSindhiya Ghat se Gwaliar Ghat Tak
19. Yatra Mangala Gauri Ghat se Hanuman Gadhi Ghat Tak
20. Yatra Gaay Ghat Se Nishad Ghat Tak
21. MAA GANGA, GHATEN EVM UTSAV
22. Ganga Arti Dev Deepavali evam Any Utsav
23. Potentials of Digitalized India
24. VEDIC CONSCIOUSNESS
25. A Brief Introduction to Vedic Science
26. Kashi ke Barah Jyotirling
27. IMPACT OF MOTIVATION
28. Let's have a Milky Way Journey
29. Color Therapy in a Nutshell

90. Astrological Remedies
91. The Secret Power of Motivation
92. Secret of Developing your Inner Strength
93. The Secret Path to Motivation
94. The Art and Secret of Positive Thinking
95. The Secrets of Practicing Ethical Living
96. Indian Art and Painting
97. The Indian Herbalism
98. Bharatanatyam to Kathak
99. Exploring India's Astrological Remedies
100. The Indian Festival of Flowers
101. Indian Handicrafts
102. The Splashes of Joy – India's Colour Festival
103. The Indian Science of Astrology
104. The Indian Mythology
105. Path to Enlightenment
106. The Indian Spirituality for Children
107. Aromas of India
108. The Secrets of Healthy Relationships
109. Ancestral Ties
110. The Indian Street Food
111. Discovering America
112. The Indian Textile
113. Listening to Motivational Speeches
114. Taste of India
115. A Cultural Journey through Indian Nuptials
116. Motivational Quote for Change
117. Secret Strategies for Making Money
118. Secrets to Cultivate a Positive Mindset
119. A Tapestry of Cultures: Exploring India from Kashmir to Kanyakumari
120. Achieving Your Dreams with Resilience: Secret Strategies for Overcoming Obstacles

Contact

DR. JAGADEESH PILLAI

MBA & PhD in Vedic Science

Four Times Guinness World Record Holder

Winner of Mahatma Gandhi Vishwa Shanti Puraskar and
Global Peace Ambassador

Gemology, Astro & Vastu Consultant - Spiritual Counselor

Consultant for designing World Record Ideas

Efficient Tarot Card Reader

9839093003

myrichindia@gmail.com

drjagadeeshpillai@facebook

drjagadeeshpillai@instagram
jagadeeshpillai@youtube

www. JAGADEESHPILLAI.com

|| LOKAHA SAMASTHAHA SUKHINO BHAVANTU ||